CHINESE MYTHOLOGY

Nüwa and Fuxi

Marriage and Creation Deities

BY HEATHER C. HUDAK

CONTENT CONSULTANT
GANG LIU, PhD
ASSOCIATE TEACHING PROFESSOR
CARNEGIE MELLON UNIVERSITY

Kids Core
An Imprint of Abdo Publishing
abdobooks.com

abdobooks.com

Published by Abdo Publishing, a division of ABDO, PO Box 398166, Minneapolis, Minnesota 55439.

Printed in the United States of America, North Mankato, Minnesota.
102022
012023

THIS BOOK CONTAINS RECYCLED MATERIALS

Cover Photo: Pictures from History/Universal Images Group/Getty Images
Interior Photos: Shutterstock Images, 4–5, 8, 23; Pictures From History/Universal Images Group/Getty Images, 6, 14, 28 (top), 29 (bottom); Yogi Black/Alamy, 10, 12–13; Kayana Sol/Shutterstock Images, 16; Yin Zhong/Xinhua News Agency/Getty Images, 18–19; Visual China Group/Getty Images, 20; Pictures From History/CPA Media Pte Ltd/Alamy, 21, 28 (bottom); Costfoto/Future Publishing/Getty Images, 24; Xiao Zhengqiang/Xinhua/Alamy, 26, 29 (top)

Editor: Ann Schwab
Series Designer: Ryan Gale

Library of Congress Control Number: 2022940653

Publisher's Cataloging-in-Publication Data

Names: Hudak, Heather C., author.
Title: Nüwa and Fuxi: Marriage and Creation Deities / by Heather C. Hudak
Description: Minneapolis, Minnesota: Abdo Publishing, 2023 | Series: Chinese Mythology | Includes online resources and index.
Identifiers: ISBN 9781532199974 (lib. bdg.) | ISBN 9781098275174 (ebook)
Subjects: LCSH: Deities--Juvenile literature. | Gods, Chinese--Juvenile literature. | Mythology, Chinese--Juvenile literature.
Classification: DDC 299.51--dc23

CONTENTS

Pangu, the Chinese creation god, separated heaven and Earth.

CHAPTER 1

Bonded for Life

In the beginning, heaven and Earth were connected. Pangu, the creation god, split them apart. After Pangu died, his body became the sun, moon, and stars. It also formed parts of Earth. His blood became rivers. His muscles turned into soil.

Nüwa, *left*, and Fuxi are folk heroes in China.

The goddess Huaxu came to Earth from heaven. She wanted to explore this new world. As she was walking, she stepped into the footprint of Leishen, the god of thunder. He was a very powerful god. By stepping into his footprint, she became **pregnant**. She had twins. She named the girl Nüwa and the boy Fuxi.

Nüwa and Fuxi lived on Earth. But there were no other beings on the planet. They wondered if they could marry. They climbed to the top of Kunlun Mountain. It was a **sacred** place, close to heaven. Then they asked the gods to let them marry.

Images of the moon and sun are often used to explain the concept of yin and yang.

As they prayed, two columns of smoke and clouds rose to heaven. The two columns came together. Nüwa and Fuxi took it as a sign they should get married.

Ancient China

China is one of the oldest civilizations on Earth. People began to form civilizations in China in about 5,000 BCE. Many small communities came together to create one powerful empire.

The people shared deep **cultural** beliefs. They told stories to explain the world around them. Many tales were about nature.

Yin and Yang

In ancient China, people believed everything had an opposite. These opposites must be balanced to keep order and harmony. For instance, the sun and moon, and male and female are traditionally thought of as opposites. This concept is known as yin and yang. Nüwa and Fuxi often represent yin and yang. Nüwa holds a compass as a symbol of heaven. Fuxi holds a square as a symbol of Earth.

This carving of Nüwa and Fuxi, pictured along with twin dragons, dates back to the Eastern Han dynasty (25–220 CE).

Some stories were based on real life and historical events. Others were folktales or legends. This collection of stories is called Chinese mythology.

Chinese mythology has been passed down for thousands of years. Many myths are religious. They often feature **deities**. Nüwa and Fuxi were some of the first and most important deities.

PRIMARY SOURCE

Nüwa and Fuxi have been quoted in literature asking the gods for permission to marry:

> If Heaven allows us to be man and wife,
>
> please let the smoke before us gather;
>
> if not, please let the smoke scatter.

Source: *Transnational Chinese Cinemas: Identity, Nationhood, Gender*, edited by Sheldon Hsiao-peng Lu, University of Hawaii Press, 1997, books.google.ca. Accessed 6 May 2022.

Comparing Texts

Think about the quote. Does it support the information in this chapter? Or does it give a different perspective? Explain how in a few sentences.

There are several different stories about how Fuxi, *pictured*, and Nüwa were born.

CHAPTER 2

Ancient Origins

Sometimes, Nüwa and Fuxi are shown as husband and wife. Other times, they are brother and sister. There are many stories about their origins. They don't all say that Huaxu was their mother.

Nüwa, *pictured*, and Fuxi are sometimes shown as part human and part serpent.

Some myths say Nüwa and Fuxi were the only survivors of a great flood. They were often shown as part human and part serpent.

Their tails were wound around each other to show their close bond.

The First Humans

Ancient myths tell how Nüwa created the first humans. She took handfuls of clay and shaped them into humans. Nüwa used her powers to bring the clay lumps to life. But she soon grew tired of making each human by hand.

A Fitting Name

Nüwa is honored as the Great Mother Goddess for her role in creating humans. Her name is written in the Chinese language as 女媧. It begins with the Chinese character for woman, nǚ (女). It ends with a character that belongs only to her, wā (媧).

Nüwa protected the people she had created by fixing a huge hole in the sky. Nüwa patched the hole using a potion made from five different-colored stones she had received from the gods.

Nüwa dipped a rope in the clay. Then, she swung the rope in the air. Lumps of clay flew all around her. Each lump became a human.

The humans Nüwa shaped by hand were wealthy and powerful. The humans that came from the clay lumps were lower or middle class. Some of the mud and clay people melted in the rain. This was how sickness and disease came to be.

Later myths tell how Fuxi helped Nüwa mold humans from clay. Nüwa and Fuxi became known as the parents of humankind.

Further Evidence

Look at the website below. Does it give any new evidence to support Chapter Two?

Mythology

abdocorelibrary.com/nuwa-and-fuxi

Many Chinese wedding traditions, such as the bride covering her face, began with Nüwa and Fuxi.

CHAPTER 3

Powerful Pair

Nüwa and Fuxi are great cultural heroes in Chinese mythology. Together, they invented the concept of marriage. They began the tradition of praying before a wedding. They also offered sacrifices to the gods before the ceremony.

A giant stone statue of Fuxi's face has been carved out of Xianshan Mountain, outside Xiangyang, China.

Fuxi put rules in place for a marriage. One of them was that men should marry at the age of 30. But Fuxi felt women should marry at age 20.

Helping People on Earth

Fuxi did not play a big role in creating humans. But he found many ways to improve their lives. He gave people the tools and skills they needed to thrive.

Fuxi made many important contributions to Chinese society.

Hunting used a lot of energy. Fuxi taught humans how to fish and farm the land instead. He also showed them how to tame wild animals to use for milk, meat, and eggs.

Fuxi invented writing, music, cooking, and **currency**. He showed people how to weave silkworm thread into fabric. He taught them to use water from the Yellow River to **irrigate** the land.

Fuxi also created the bagua. It is made up of eight sections. Each section has three stacked broken or unbroken lines that stand for yin and yang. These lines symbolize different parts of the natural world. A balance of all parts is needed to keep order.

The Bagua

Fuxi was inspired to make the bagua after seeing the pattern on the back of a tortoise shell. The Early Heaven version of the bagua, *above*, is also called the Primordial Bagua.

A festival celebrating Nüwa is held in Shexian County, Hebei Province, China.

Nüwa is worshipped as the Great Mother Goddess. Nüwa's main role in Chinese myths was to care for her children and all the people of Earth. One myth tells how she saved the world from a great flood. Two gods were fighting and created a huge hole in the sky. Rain poured through it. Nüwa used a potion made from stones to patch the hole.

Corners of the Sky

Heaven and Earth did not line up exactly after Nüwa fixed the sky. Ancient Chinese people believed this was the reason why Earth is tilted. It also explained why the rivers in China flow southwest and the sun, moon, and stars move northwest.

A ceremony at Fuxi Temple in Tianshui City, China, honors the god and his place in Chinese culture.

Nüwa and Fuxi Today

Both Nüwa and Fuxi are still worshipped today. There are many temples built in honor of them across China. Wahuang Palace in Handan is the largest place of worship dedicated to Nüwa. It was built more than 1,400 years ago on the side of Fenghuang Mountain.

Fuxi's tomb is in Huaiyang County, in Henan Province. It was built about 3,000 years ago. Today, it is a sacred place. Festivals are held for these gods each year. People respect Nüwa and Fuxi as heroes. They honor them for their important roles in Chinese culture and history.

Explore Online

Visit the website below. Does it give any new information about the Wahuang Palace that was not in Chapter Three?

Wahuang Palace

abdocorelibrary.com/nuwa-and-fuxi

LEGENDARY FACTS

Nüwa is worshipped as the Great Mother Goddess.

Fuxi invented music, writing, cooking, and currency.

Festivals in China honor Nüwa and Fuxi.

Nüwa and Fuxi represent the concept of yin and yang.

Glossary

cultural
having to do with traditions, beliefs, customs, and art that are shared by a group of people

currency
money

deities
gods or goddesses

irrigate
supply farmland with water

pregnant
carrying a growing, unborn baby

sacred
holy; a place of worship

Online Resources

To learn more about Nüwa, Fuxi, and Chinese mythology, visit our free resource websites below.

Core Library
CONNECTION
FREE! COMMON CORE MULTIMEDIA RESOURCES

Visit **abdocorelibrary.com** or scan this QR code for free Common Core resources for teachers and students, including vetted activities, multimedia, and booklinks, for deeper subject comprehension.

Booklinks
NONFICTION NETWORK
FREE! ONLINE NONFICTION RESOURCES

Visit **abdobooklinks.com** or scan this QR code for free additional online weblinks for further learning. These links are routinely monitored and updated to provide the most current information available.

Learn More

Fu, Shelley. *Chinese Myths and Legends: The Monkey King and Other Adventures.* Tuttle, 2018.

Yip, Mingmei. *Chinese Children's Favorite Stories: Fables, Myths, and Fairy Tales.* Tuttle, 2020.

Index

About the Author

Heather C. Hudak has written hundreds of kids' books on all kinds of topics. She loves to travel when she's not writing. Heather has visited about 60 countries, including China. She also enjoys camping with her husband and many pets.